My Style

I love creating intricate black and white floral designs that start with focal points such as animals, faces, inspirational quotes, or mandalas. I always begin with a subject in mind, then add botanical details in the background. Some of my pieces are inspired by famous buildings around the world, and others are works of fantasy-inspired doodle art featuring forests, parks, waterfalls, etc. And I can't get enough of bold and bright colors on my drawings!

My Favorite Coloring Supplies

Here's a quick look at some of my preferred coloring media. But don't forget! You can also use crayons, water-based markers, gel pens . . . anything you like!

A. Fine-point felt-tip pens: Some of us love adding patterns on drawings while coloring; felt-tip pens are great for that. They are also good for adding colors inside small, detailed areas.

B. Colored pencils: For a smooth coloring experience, I highly recommend colored pencils. They are very easy to blend and great for layering colors.

C. Brush markers: These are your best choice if you want to achieve bright and vivid colors. Depending on the brand you use, they are very blendable. My favorites are Winsor & Newton and Copic Sketch markers.

D. Chisel-tip markers: These are good for coloring large areas. With the various angles of the tip, you can get three types of stroke: broad, medium, and thin. Colorless chisel-tip markers are also great to use as a blending tool.

E. Water-soluble pastels: If you want to add a splash of watercolor to your designs, use water-soluble pastels. They act like crayons when dry, but you have the option of applying water to add a watercolor wash to your work, and they are very easy to manipulate. You can even use an alcohol-based blender marker or a paper blending stump to blend the colors.

B. Prismacolor colored pencils

A. BIC markers

D. Copic Original markers

A. Stabilo fine point pens

E. Caran d'Ache Neocolor water-soluble pastels

C. Copic Sketch markers

B. Prismacolor colored pencils

Coloring Tips

Choose a color palette if you're unsure of what colors to use. There are tons of color palettes online, or let a photo or object inspire you! For this design, I selected a mini palette for different areas of the design and put them all together to make sure they'd work well.

Don't be afraid to mix and match colors!

White gel pens are great to use for adding highlights, or to add patterning on top of a dark color.

If I am going for a fun and vibrant look, I mix multiple coloring media in one design— alcohol-based markers, colored pencils, crayons, water-soluble pastels, water-based markers, and gel pens.

How to Blend

I'm always going for the well-blended look. To achieve this, I use a good blender, though you can also blend without a blender by simply using several different shades of a single color and building up a gradient with them. But I like to use an **alcohol-based blender marker** with almost every coloring medium and design that I do. Blenders with chiseled tips are my favorite because they are versatile—you can get thick and thin lines and blends out of them. I usually begin with light pastel shades no matter what medium I'm using. That way I can slowly build the colors to bright, bold tones.

1. Fill the center of the flower with a light color, like this yellow.

2. Now use a darker color to go around the inner edges of the flower center, on top of the light color.

3. Blend the colors using a blending tool such as a blending marker, using gentle strokes and moving your tool from dark to light.

4. Fill in the petals with a new light color, like this orange.

5. Now use a darker color, like this dark orange, around the outer edges of the center of the flower.

6. This darker color at the base of the petals gives the flower dimensional, realistic "shadows."

7. Blend the colors using a blending tool such as a blending marker—chisel tips like this one are my favorite.

8. Your beautifully blended flower is done!

Coloring Leaves

When I color leafy drawings, I use many different shades of green. I also like to use two different color supplies: alcohol-based markers and colored pencils. Below, I'll walk you through my leaf process! Here are the two color palettes I used in this example.

Alcohol-based markers   *Colored pencils*

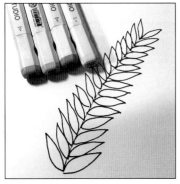

1. Pick the shades of green that you want to use.

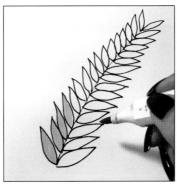

2. Start coloring with the lightest marker.

3. Pick a darker marker and begin coloring the corners of the leaves.

4. Fill in the outer corners of the leaves with the darker shade.

5. Start blending with an alcohol-based blender marker until the light and dark colors are nicely merged.

6. Color the stem or stem area with another darker green marker.

7. Use a colored pencil to add more depth to the leaves.

8. Begin tracing the outer edges of the leaves and stem with colored pencil.

9. Blend everything with the blender marker.

10. Now use a different, blue-green colored pencil around each leaf and stem.

11. Continue with the new color and blend until you're satisfied.

12. You're done!

Happy Days, page 57.

Markers (Copic, Prismacolor, Spectrum Noir), colored pencils (Prismacolor), pens (Micron). Color by Lisa Caryl.

You Are Good Enough

Good Enough, page 47.
Colored pencils (Prismacolor). Color by Jeannine Drevitch.

Positivity, page 21.

8   *Markers (Spectrum Noir, Staedtler), colored pencils (Prismacolor), pens (Micron). Color by Lisa Caryl.*

A Free Life, page 39.
Markers (Chameleon, Ironlak). Color by Kati Erney.

Heart Full of Love, page 37.

10   *Colored pencils (Prismacolor). Color by Kelly Nagorka.*

Strength, page 33.
Markers (Spectrum Noir), pens (Staedtler), colored pencils (Prismacolor). Color by Lisa Caryl. 11

Stay Inspired, page 35.

12   *Markers, colored pencils (Prismacolor), blending marker (Winsor & Newton). Color by Jeannine Drevitch.*

Perseverance, page 41.

Colored pencils (Prismacolor), white gel pen (Uni-Ball). Color by Keara Irby.

Live, Love, Laugh, page 43.
Colored pencils (Faber-Castell). Color by Krisa Bousquet.

Be Happy, Be You, page 17.

16   *Colored pencils (Prismacolor). Color by Kelly Nagorka.*

Don't lose hope.
When the sun goes down,
the stars come out.

—Unknown

19

Storms make trees
take deeper roots.

—Dolly Parton

positive mind
positive vibes
positive life

Simplify and focus on the good.
The beauty of the journey ahead
will flourish on its own.

—Erik Tomblin

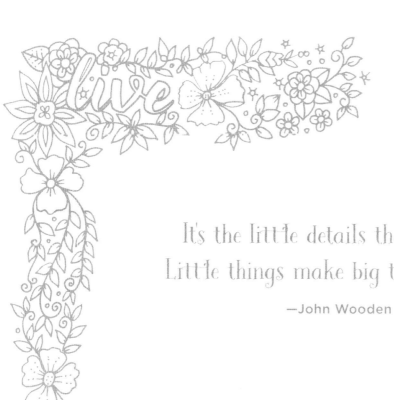

It's the little details that are vital.
Little things make big things happen.

—John Wooden

When you're true to who you are,
amazing things happen.

—Deborah Norville

_____

_____

_____

_____

_____

_____

_____

Art is not a thing;
it is a way.

—Elbert Hubbard

No beauty shines brighter
than that of a good heart.

—Unknown

Flower Flourish

The most important thing in life
is to learn how to give out love,
and to let it come in.

—Morrie Schwartz

A light green background and dark green leaves really
allow the flowers in this piece to stand out.

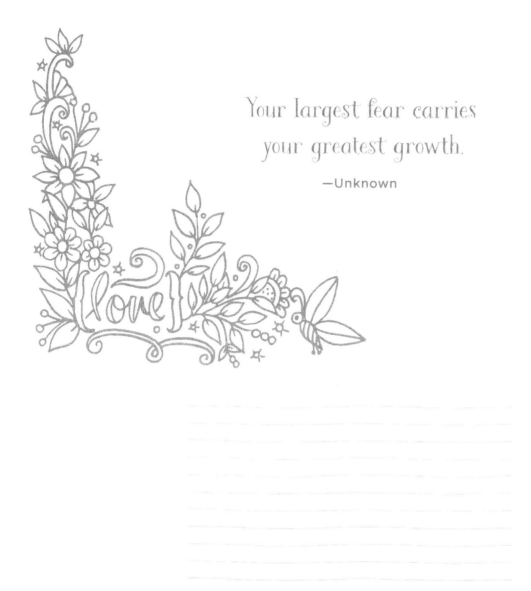

Your largest fear carries
your greatest growth.

—Unknown

Strength

Warm blooms contrast nicely
against cool green leaves and blue sky.

Stay inspired
so you can inspire.

—Unknown

Stay Inspired

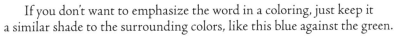

If you don't want to emphasize the word in a coloring, just keep it
a similar shade to the surrounding colors, like this blue against the green.

Love yourself first
and everything else falls into line.
You really have to love yourself
to get anything done in this world.

—Lucille Ball

Heart Full of Love

For a mandala design, try coloring
each patterned row a different color.

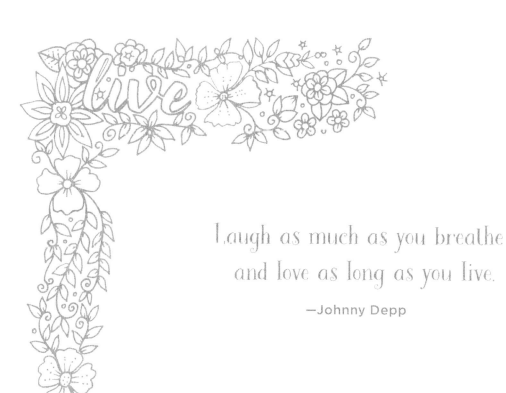

Laugh as much as you breathe
and love as long as you live.

—Johnny Depp

A Free Life

This gorgeous jewel toned piece includes tiny
but effective white highlights mixed in everywhere.

Never stop trying.
Never stop believing.
Never give up.
Your day will come.

—Mandy Hale

Perseverance

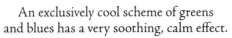

An exclusively cool scheme of greens
and blues has a very soothing, calm effect.

You are you.
Now, isn't that pleasant?

—Dr. Seuss

Live, Love, Laugh

Why not let the colors of the rainbow shine not only in the rainbow itself, but in the flowers surrounding it too?

The best way to cheer yourself up
is to try to cheer somebody else up.

—Mark Twain

Rainbow

Use different tints and shades of the same
few colors to create realistic depth in a piece.

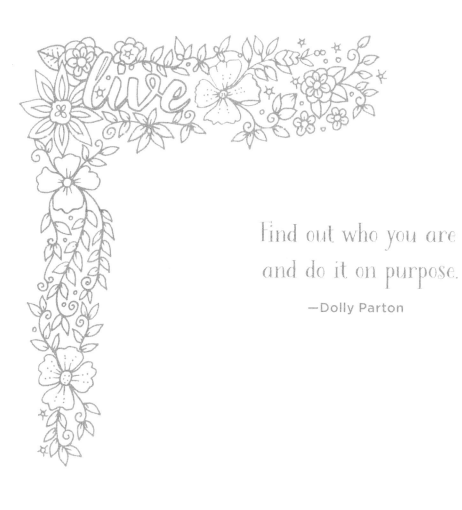

Find out who you are
and do it on purpose.

—Dolly Parton

Good Enough

Choose a job you love
and you will never work a day in your life.

—Confucius

Life is a Gift

Learn from yesterday,
live for today,
hope for tomorrow.

—Albert Einstein

Sometimes people are beautiful.
Not in looks. Not in what they say.
Just in what they are.

—Markus Zusak, *I Am the Messenger*

Life is tough, my darling,
but so are you.

—Stephanie Bennett-Henry

These days are ours
Happy and free
These days are ours
Share them with me.

—Norman Gimbel, "Happy Days"

Motivation is everything.
You can do the work of two people,
but you can't be two people.
Instead, you have to inspire the next guy
down the line and get him
to inspire his people.

—Lee Iacocca

make yourself proud

Fall seven times,
stand up eight.

—Japanese proverb

Be Proud

You attract the energy that you give off.
Spread good vibes.
Think positively. Enjoy life.

—Unknown

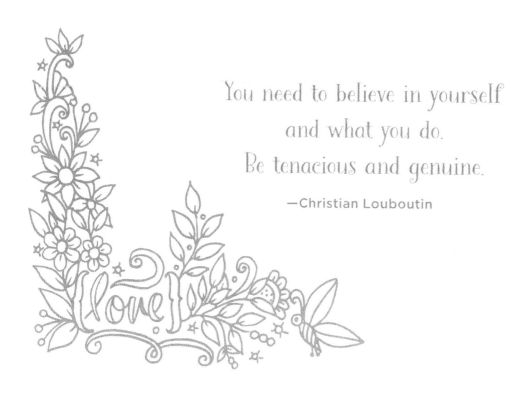

You need to believe in yourself
and what you do.
Be tenacious and genuine.

—Christian Louboutin

It's Okay Not to be Perfect

Have no fear of perfection—
you'll never reach it.

—Salvador Dalí

"No act of kindness, no matter how small, is ever wasted." - Aesop

You is kind.
You is smart.
You is important.

—Kathryn Stockett, *The Help*

A Kind Heart

Spread a little kindness along the way...

I aspire to be a giver.
A giver of love, a giver of good vibes,
and a giver of strength.

—Unknown

Find strength in Pain

kriso 2016

The pain you feel today
is the strength you feel tomorrow.
For every challenge encountered
there is opportunity for growth.

—Unknown

"Nothing Will Work Unless You Do"

-Maya Angelou

There are no secrets to success.
It is the result of preparation,
hard work, and learning from failure.

—Colin Powell

You may have to fight a battle
more than once to win it.

—Margaret Thatcher

Kind Wings